FIELD&STREAM

HOW TO CATCH BASS

FIELD & STREAM

HOW TO CATCH BASS

JOE CERMELE
AND THE EDITORS OF *FIELD & STREAM*

weldon**owen**

CONTENTS

I WAS BORN INTO A FISHING FAMILY.

My grandparents on my mom's side owned a little bait and tackle shop in central New Jersey. My grandfather on my dad's side dragged me to every fishing hole within a 30-mile radius of home as soon as I could walk. After school in the spring and fall, my mom would drive us straight to a local lake where we'd fish together until dark, and my dad and I spent every weekend on our family boat. These days, I can say that fishing is no longer a hobby or pastime for me. It has become a physical need, as important to my mental health as getting eight hours of sleep would be for someone else.

When you're young, all you want to do is catch fish. The outing's worth is always defined by the end result. As you grow older, you come to realize that a fishing trip isn't just about what you catch, but about the conversations you have on the water and getting away from everyday life. For me, the most important thing I take away from a trip these days is knowledge. I may not have caught anything, but if I learned something new that I can use later, it was a good day.

A lot of tricks and techniques I've learned along the way can be found in these pages. Whether they were shared with me or shared with one of the many other contributors who lent their writing talent to this project, know that the book you're holding is a compilation of wisdom passed on by some of the most hard-working, fish-catching, passionate anglers on the planet.

The techniques, tactics, and tools presented in this book are aimed at giving you an edge every time you hit the water and will help you build a lifetime of fishing memories and (hopefully) a laundry list of trophy catches. However, always remember that no angler, regardless of how skilled they believe they are, will ever figure out the game so perfectly that they never fail. Fishing is a constant learning process, and that's what keeps us coming back to the water time and time again. If it were easy all the time, we probably wouldn't want to fish anymore.

Joe Cermele
Fishing Editor, *Field & Stream*

1 USE THE GREATEST LURES OF ALL TIME

When targeting bass, know the lures that actually work. It's useful to know the ones for some of your other catches, too. Some are lures your granddad fished. Others have earned their reputation for productivity in more recent decades. In all cases, you'll find a lure that catches fish, time after time.

REBEL POP-R There are lots of poppers on the market, but this one casts farther than most and spits water like no other.

MANN'S 1-MINUS This crankbait easily skims the top of barely submerged weedbeds. That's often where the bass live.

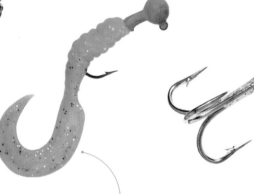

CURLY TAIL GRUB Combined with a plain or painted roundhead jig, these are arguably the most versatile fishing lures of all time.

ROOSTER TAIL For large brown and rainbow trout in bigger rivers and lakes, this is the hot-ticket lure.

PANTHER MARTIN A staple from Montana to Maine, these spinners are perfect for picking trout from the pockets of steeply tumbling mountain creeks.

YAMAMOTO SENKO The fluttering action of this soft-plastic lure as it falls is amazingly effective for large- and smallmouth bass.

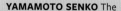

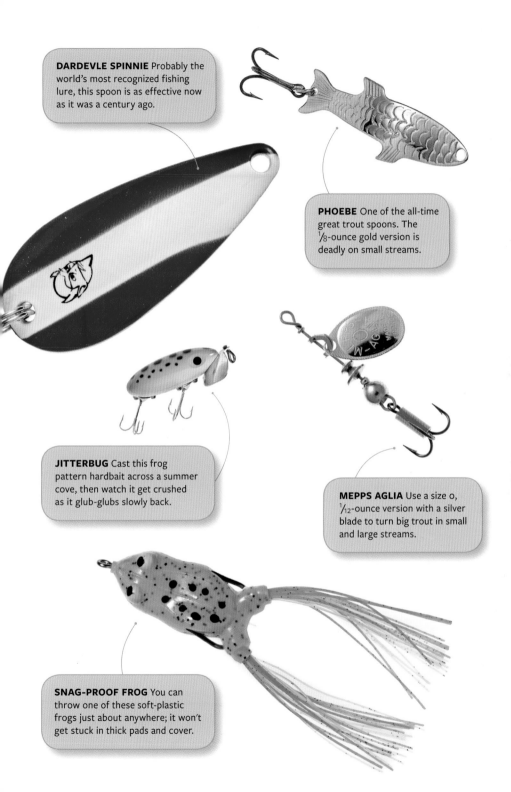

DARDEVLE SPINNIE Probably the world's most recognized fishing lure, this spoon is as effective now as it was a century ago.

PHOEBE One of the all-time great trout spoons. The 1/8-ounce gold version is deadly on small streams.

JITTERBUG Cast this frog pattern hardbait across a summer cove, then watch it get crushed as it glub-glubs slowly back.

MEPPS AGLIA Use a size 0, 1/12-ounce version with a silver blade to turn big trout in small and large streams.

SNAG-PROOF FROG You can throw one of these soft-plastic frogs just about anywhere; it won't get stuck in thick pads and cover.

2 MEET THE NEW CLASSICS

They're definitely not your father's lures (but he'll probably want to borrow them from you). These crankbaits, soft plastics, and jigs—plus some that are in categories all their own—are the hottest baits on bass impoundments, walleye lakes, and trout streams today. And we're betting anglers will be tying them on for decades, because what they do is catch fish consistently. Start making some room in your tackle box.

GULP! MINNOW If a fish eats baitfish, it'll also eat a Gulp! Minnow. This versatile soft bait comes in a range of sizes.

ZOOM FLUKE The Fluke is at its best when rigged weedless and worked in a twitch-fall pattern off the bottom.

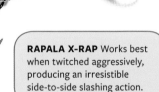

RAPALA X-RAP Works best when twitched aggressively, producing an irresistible side-to-side slashing action.

REBEL CRICKHOPPER This cricket-shaped crankbait flat-out slays every summer fish from panfish to trout to bass.

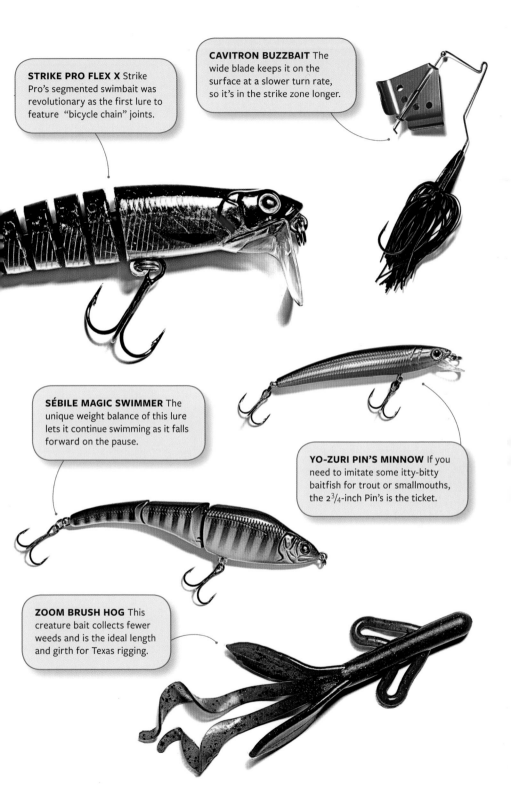

STRIKE PRO FLEX X Strike Pro's segmented swimbait was revolutionary as the first lure to feature "bicycle chain" joints.

CAVITRON BUZZBAIT The wide blade keeps it on the surface at a slower turn rate, so it's in the strike zone longer.

SÉBILE MAGIC SWIMMER The unique weight balance of this lure lets it continue swimming as it falls forward on the pause.

YO-ZURI PIN'S MINNOW If you need to imitate some itty-bitty baitfish for trout or smallmouths, the $2^3/_4$-inch Pin's is the ticket.

ZOOM BRUSH HOG This creature bait collects fewer weeds and is the ideal length and girth for Texas rigging.

3 SECURE YOUR LURE

Put a drop of superglue on your hook or jighead shank before threading on any soft-plastic lure. The instant bond will prevent the lure from slipping back on the hook with repeated casting. Soft plastics that slip down on the hook can quickly lose their enticing action and they must often be discarded long before they are actually worn out.

4 USE AN IRRESISTIBLE JIG

Summertime bass love to hang out on deep humps, ledges, and dropoffs covered with gravel, rocks, or shell beds. This is true whether you're after spots, largemouths, or smallies in a reservoir or a natural lake. This type of hard, snaggy bottom eats regular jigs like potato chips, but a wide football-head jig scurries over this bottom structure easily. Even better, a football jig appeals to the biggest bass in school.

HEADS AND TAILS A $^{1}/_{2}$- or $^{3}/_{4}$-ounce skirted football jig grinds on the bottom. This attracts bass and goads strikes, And you can feel every pebble. Dress the jig with a 4-inch twin curly-tail or plastic craw. Go with black-and-blue in stained water and green pumpkin in clear water.

TOUCH DOWN Cast a football jig with a 7-foot medium-heavy baitcasting outfit matched up with 14-pound fluorocarbon line. The long, stiff rod will take up slack on the hookset, and the low-stretch fluorocarbon sinks, thus allowing the jig to keep contact with the for more solid hookups.

INTERCEPTION Drag the jig slowly over the bottom by pulling the rod sideways to roll the hook and trailer up, making the bait a perfect imitation of a fleeing crawdad. You should feel the jig tickling a hard washboard bottom. When that sensation changes to a steady weight, set the hook.

5 RIG ME SOFTLY

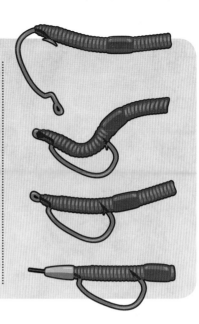

CAROLINA RIG To make this common rig for bottom dredging, Texas-rig a worm or lizard but leave the hook eye exposed. Tie 18 inches of clear leader between the hook and a small barrel swivel. On your main line, thread a brass Carolina weight (or lead sinker), followed by a small red glass bead, and tie your main line to the other side of the swivel. The weight will click against the glass bead as you fish to help attract bass.

6 CATCH BIG BASS WITH BUNNY FUR

Pork rinds and curly-tailed grubs are excellent trailers for jigs and spinnerbaits, but when pro angler Dave Wolak needs to up his game, he steals a page from the flyfisherman's book and hooks on a bunny strip. "The fluttering action looks just like a mouse tail," he says. The pennant of rabbit skin, typically used on streamer patterns, also won't come off easily.

7 HARVEST NATURE'S BAIT BOUNTY

If you have a shovel and a lawn, you've got all the worms you need. But that's not the only productive bait around. The creek you fish can supply its own—for free. (Just be sure to check bait-collection regulations in your area before heading out.)

Good bait shops carry some of these critters, but expect to pay at least $17 for a dozen hellgrammites, $5 for 12 shiners, and $3 a pound for crayfish.

HELLGRAMMITES Most fish love these nasty aquatic larvae. You can pick them off the bottom of submerged rocks by hand, or stretch a seine across a fast-water section of the creek and flip rocks upstream. The current will flush the bugs into the net.

MINNOWS They're easier to catch off the main current, so approach from midstream with a seine and corral the school against the bank as the net closes. If the bait is thick and the water fairly shallow, a quick swipe with a long-handled dip net will work too.

CRAYFISH Find a stretch of slow-to-moderate current, and then flip rocks and scoop up crayfish with a dip net. You can also stretch a seine across the creek and walk downstream to it while splashing around and kicking rocks over to spook crayfish into the mesh.

SALAMANDERS Often overlooked, this bait is like catnip to bass and big trout. Find them under larger rocks near the water's edge. Good rocks are often dry on top but cool and moist underneath. Moss-covered rocks farther up the bank are also good.

GRUBS Find rotten logs or wood near a creek bed. Peel away the bark to expose the soft, dead wood, or dig in the dirt underneath, and you'll likely find some fat white grubs. Finding a trout or crappie that won't eat them? Impossible!

GRASSHOPPERS The best way to catch hoppers is to walk through the tall grass that often flanks a stream with a cheap butterfly net. Just skim the net across the tips of the blades; you'll have a dozen or more hoppers in a flash.

8 MAKE SPOOKS SPOOKIER

The Heddon Zara Spook, a stogie-shaped, dog-walking stickbait, has been duping bass for more than 70 years. Heddon offers several versions, but the 5-inch, ⅞-ounce Super Spook is the favorite of legendary pro bass angler Penny Berryman. Berryman performs several modifications that turn her Super Spook into a "Superb" Spook, and it would take a Brink's truck to haul all the money Berryman has won with this lure. Her tweaked lure is 4⅜ inches long and weighs about ¾ ounce—almost the size of the original Zara Spook. However, her Superb Spook is even stouter, and it presents a better profile and splashes more when walked across the surface.

STEP 1 Remove the hooks. Mark off a 5/8-inch-wide section of the lure around the middle hook hanger. The mark on the nose side should be about 1/4 inch from the split-ring hanger. Then saw off the marked section. Save the split ring and put it on the line eye to give the bait freedom to sashay.

STEP 2 Place two small ball bearings, six BBs, or two 8-mm glass beads inside the lure. They'll rattle and make the lure's tail sit deeper for better hookups. Apply a coat of 5-minute epoxy with a toothpick to the sawed openings on each half of the lure. Let the epoxy set.

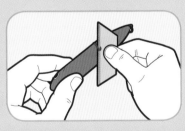

STEP 3 Shave off the excess epoxy with a razor. Sand the joint smooth with 220-grit sandpaper and finish it off with a buffing compound. Replace the hooks with longer-shaft Gamakatsu hooks. A red front treble reduces short strikes by encouraging bass to attack the head of the bait.

9 BUILD A BUDGET LURE

During the Great Depression, hard-up anglers crafted lures out of scrap wood and metal like this Copper Tube bait, which once filled tackle boxes across the nation and can be built on the cheap. These directions are for a bass lure, but you can make it in different sizes to catch everything from panfish to pike, and even muskies. For saltwater species, just substitute PVC pipe. Here's how to make your own.

1. Place a 2 3/4-inch section of 1/2-inch-diameter copper plumbing pipe in a vise. Cut the front end of the pipe at a 45-degree angle.

2. Sand each end to remove burrs that could nick fishing line.

3. Drill two 1/2-inch holes (top front and bottom rear), and again remove burrs.

4. At this point, the lure will the lure will sink slowly. If you want it to sink faster, seal the back with caulk, let it dry, drop in three No. 5 split shot, and caulk the front. Now it'll rattle, too.

5. Remove excess caulk and clean the lure, then mask the lower half of the body and spray black paint across the top.

6. Superglue an eye (available at hobby shops) on each side of the front. Once set, spray the lure with lacquer.

7. Add a split ring to the front and a sharp treble hook to the rear.

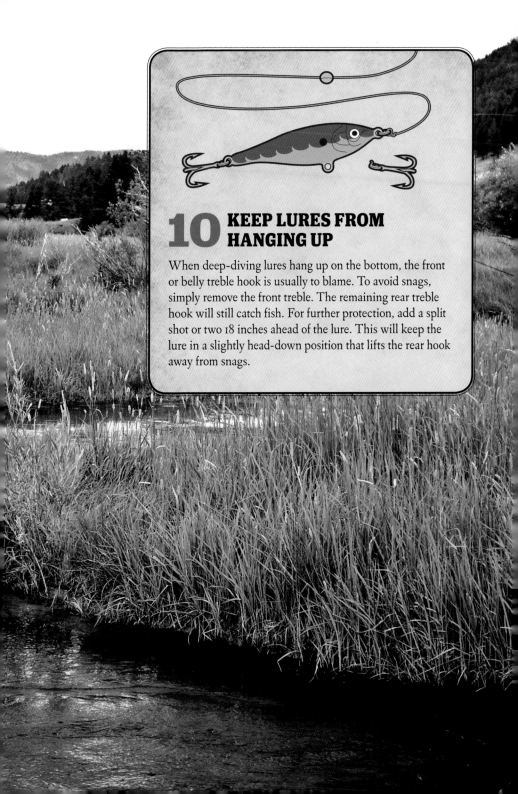

10 KEEP LURES FROM HANGING UP

When deep-diving lures hang up on the bottom, the front or belly treble hook is usually to blame. To avoid snags, simply remove the front treble. The remaining rear treble hook will still catch fish. For further protection, add a split shot or two 18 inches ahead of the lure. This will keep the lure in a slightly head-down position that lifts the rear hook away from snags.

11 MAKE OVER LURES WITH TOOTHPASTE

An occasional cleaning with toothpaste can make your lures sparkle like new. It has a brightening agent and mild abrasives that restore them to their original finish. Rinse yours in warm water and then scrub them gently with a soft-bristled toothbrush and toothpaste. This is particularly effective on spoons with a brass, copper, gold, or silver finish, which become much less attractive to fish when dull.

12 DO DIY CUSTOM LURE COLORS

Permanent-ink felt-tipped markers are great for making on-the-scene pattern repairs to plastic fishing lures and for increasing their visibility under specific light conditions. Use black or blue to draw distinct scale patterns or vivid dark-light contrasts. Red is good for adding bright gill slashes. Make glaring eyes with yellow and black. Carry a few colors in your tackle box.

13 FISH THE BEST FRESHWATER BAITS

Not sure what to buy at the tackle shop? You can't go wrong with one of these top producers.

CRAYFISH These freshwater crustaceans, best fished in rocky areas, are candy to bass, walleyes, and perch. You can use a whole live crayfish or just the tail meat.

GIZZARD SHAD A live adult gizzard shad makes an excellent bait for trophy freshwater pike, muskies, striped bass, and even blue and flathead catfish.

SHINERS "Shiner" is used to refer to any silver- or gold-scaled baitfish species. Use large golden shiners for largemouth bass or pike, smaller ones for trout, crappies, and smallies.

14 GIVE NEW LIFE TO OLD BASS LURES

Every bass angler owns a magical plug or crankbait that catches fish when others can't. It's critical that you take extra care of these MVPs in order to keep them from losing their mojo. Tennessee bass pro Craig Powers has been duping bass for decades with his "antique" P70 Rebel Pop-Rs; his "bass body shop" restores about 2,000 lures a year. Here's how Powers says you can keep your lures from needing an overhaul.

STOP RUST BEFORE IT STARTS
Corroded split rings are a major reason you end up with rusty hooks and discolored finishes. Powers replaces factory split rings with noncorrosive stainless-steel split rings. He also stores his prize baits in flat utility boxes to keep them from banging against one another, which chips the finish. Line the bottom of each slot with a piece of ½-inch-thick hard craft foam for added protection.

FRESHEN UP Remove rust stains and restore dull finishes by polishing baits with ketchup.

15 TIE A FIVE-MINUTE FLY

The Woolly Bugger is the perfect pattern for a learning fly-tier. It's big, so you can see what you're doing, and it requires only a few inexpensive materials. Most importantly, it's a proven producer for trout, bass, and almost anything in between. The savvy angler always has at least a few Buggers in the fly box.

STEP 1 Wrap a piece of black 6/0 thread along the length of a size 10 elongated hook. Always wrap the thread away from yourself, over the top of the hook.

STEP 2 Secure one large black marabou feather at the front of the hook and wrap all the way back to the bend. You want to leave enough exposed to create a tail.

STEP 3 Connect a 2-inch piece of fine copper wire by the tail and also a strand of black chenille. Wrap the thread forward then the chenille, but leave the wire behind. Tie off the chenille with a half hitch.

STEP 4 Now tie on a saddle hackle feather (black or grizzly), palmer it back (i.e., wrap with spacing), and secure this with a couple of wraps of the wire. Trim the leftover hackle. Wrap the wire forward and tie it off with the thread. Trim the excess wire.

STEP 5 Finish the fly with a tapered thread head. Use a whip- finish knot, apply a dab of head cement, and you're done.

16

MATCH YOUR FLUOROCARBON TO YOUR FISH

If you're fishing for largemouths in thick cover or stripers around underwater rocks, a fluorocarbon leader will fend off abrasion. When I'm nymphing for trout, I often add 3 feet of 5X or 6X fluorocarbon tippet to a standard tapered-nylon leader. The nylon butt stays at or near the surface to make control of the drifting fly easier, while the fluorocarbon tippet sinks readily with the nymph and is less evident to fussy trout. I don't use fluoro tippet to fish dries because it will sink and pull the fly underwater. For bass and walleye fishing with spinning or baitcasting gear, I like superbraid lines because of the acute sensitivity their low stretch affords. All superbraids are opaque and require the addition of a clear leader, for which fluorocarbon is almost perfect. Attaching 3 feet of 12- to 20-pound clear fluorocarbon to 50-pound superbraid gives me a more abrasion-resistant leader that fish will have a tough time seeing. The only flaw in the equation comes when I am working surface lures, for which fast-sinking fluoro is a disaster.

17

KNOW YOUR: LARGEMOUTH BASS

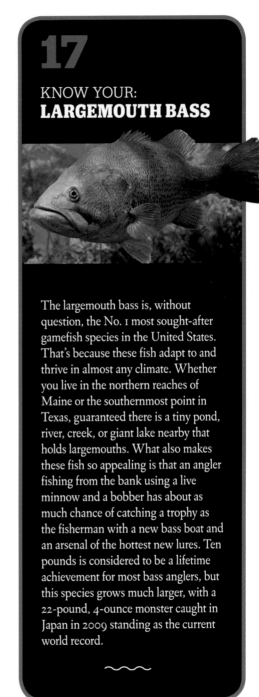

The largemouth bass is, without question, the No. 1 most sought-after gamefish species in the United States. That's because these fish adapt to and thrive in almost any climate. Whether you live in the northern reaches of Maine or the southernmost point in Texas, guaranteed there is a tiny pond, river, creek, or giant lake nearby that holds largemouths. What also makes these fish so appealing is that an angler fishing from the bank using a live minnow and a bobber has about as much chance of catching a trophy as the fisherman with a new bass boat and an arsenal of the hottest new lures. Ten pounds is considered to be a lifetime achievement for most bass anglers, but this species grows much larger, with a 22-pound, 4-ounce monster caught in Japan in 2009 standing as the current world record.

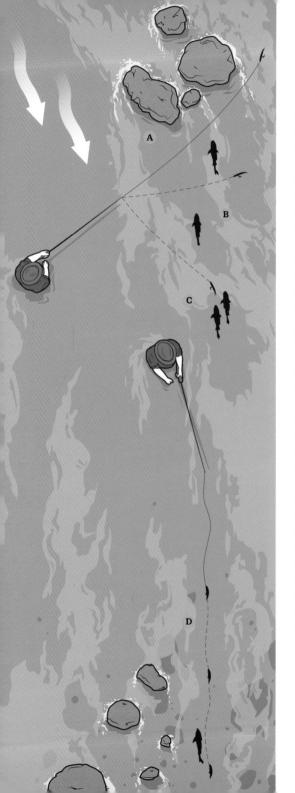

18 WADE AFTER YOUR BASS

The biggest advantage a wading angler has is the ability to stay put and pick a stretch of water apart for the most and biggest smallmouths, as opposed to getting a few fleeting casts from a drifting boat. Just don't risk injury or worse at the mercy of swift current; if you're not comfortable reaching a spot, skip it.

Here's the most practical and efficient way to ensure that you can comprehensively cover the stream eddies where smallmouths like to station themselves and feed. Position yourself three-quarters of the way up the eddy closer to the head. From here, you'll be able to make four different presentations with a spinner, crankbait, or jig in a single cast. Start by casting upstream of the eddy head (A) and working the lure downcurrent. After a few cranks, as your line is pulled along the eddy, work the lure straight across.

Turn the reel handle a few more times and stop, allowing the lure to swing down toward the eddy's tail (B), then retrieve straight upcurrent for the recast (C). In this manner, your lure is presented down, across, on the swing, then directly upcurrent in one sweep, and you can quickly determine which presentation the bass like best.

19 GO, SPEED RACER (SAFELY)

Today's bass boat is a modern marvel of efficiency—incredibly fast, stable, and smooth on the water. The fastest bass boats are capable of speeds in excess of 75 mph, but it takes skill and seat time to drive them well. Here's how to pilot your rig safely from a dead stop to top speed.

First, have your boat dealer's service center adjust the steering to remove any "slop" (excessive play) in the wheel and make sure that the engine height is right for your specific boat-outboard-propeller combination. Next, adjust the gear in your boat so that the load is evenly distributed. If you skip out on any of this, you're likely to have some handling problems.

Now get onto a big, calm body of water away from boat traffic. Fasten your outboard's kill switch to your life jacket. Crank up the engine, trim it all the way under, and when the coast is clear, accelerate. The bow will rise, then fall, as the boat gets "out of the hole" and on plane. Continue to accelerate while applying power trim judiciously to lift the bow. Be very careful not to overtrim!

As you practice getting a bass boat to speed, instead of running in a straight line, try piloting the boat in a gradual, sweeping arc to the left. This will counter the propeller's torque, and should make balancing the boat on its pad easier.

20 REIGN IN THE RAIN

If bass refuse to belt your spinnerbait during a rain shower, they may be guarding beds and unwilling to chase the lure. While it's harder to see the beds through a rain-rippled surface, the bass also have trouble seeing you. This makes them less inclined to spook and more likely to bite. Take advantage of this situation by pitching a 3½-inch tube into beds. One favored color combo is chip gold (flake) and watermelon, rigged Texas-style with a 3/0 offset hook, a 3/16-ounce bullet sinker, and 17-pound line. The heavy line will help wrestle bass out of beds nestled in nasty cover.

21 DIAGNOSE AND CURE A SICK MOTOR

Among the many early signs of spring is the fisherman standing at a boat dock, having just launched his boat for the first time after winter storage. All too often, he's scratching his head and wondering why in hell his outboard motor won't start. Here are some troubleshooting tips and tricks for anyone with a basic set of tools and rudimentary tinkering skills.

SLOW TO START First, make sure your starting battery isn't dead. Next, check that the kill switch is in the "run" position. The kill switch itself may have become corroded slightly over the winter. Corroded electrical connections are a common problem. When you find a wire terminal that's green and crusty, it's time to clean or replace it. Next, check the battery-cable connections to the engine block and starter solenoid and the fuse panel. You may have a blown fuse. Then give the rest of the boat's electrical wiring a onceover. Finally, don't make one of the most common mistakes—forgetting to open the vent on your fuel tank.

ROUGH AT IDLE While the motor is idling, turn the low-speed jet screw in and out for a bit on each carburetor to loosen any debris. See your service manual for jet-screw locations and factory settings. If this doesn't do it, there might be an ignition problem. Clean or replace spark plugs as needed. When I first start my motor, I always check to make sure there's a telltale stream of cooling water being discharged from the rear. If that stream isn't happening, the motor has to be shut down immediately before it overheats.

DEATH AT SPEED Sometimes a motor that seems to idle just fine at the dock will surge or just plain die when you're getting underway at midrange rpm. While running the motor in the problem rpm range, have a buddy rapidly squeeze the fuel-primer bulb a few times. If this extra shot of fuel smooths the motor out, then you've got a fuel delivery problem. It might be as simple as a partly clogged fuel filter, which can be an easy fix.

22 KEEP YOUR FOOTING

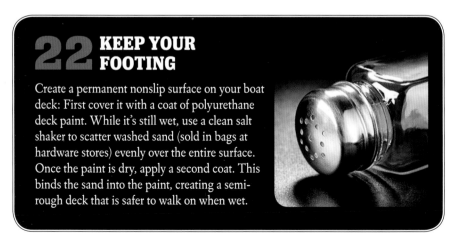

Create a permanent nonslip surface on your boat deck: First cover it with a coat of polyurethane deck paint. While it's still wet, use a clean salt shaker to scatter washed sand (sold in bags at hardware stores) evenly over the entire surface. Once the paint is dry, apply a second coat. This binds the sand into the paint, creating a semi-rough deck that is safer to walk on when wet.

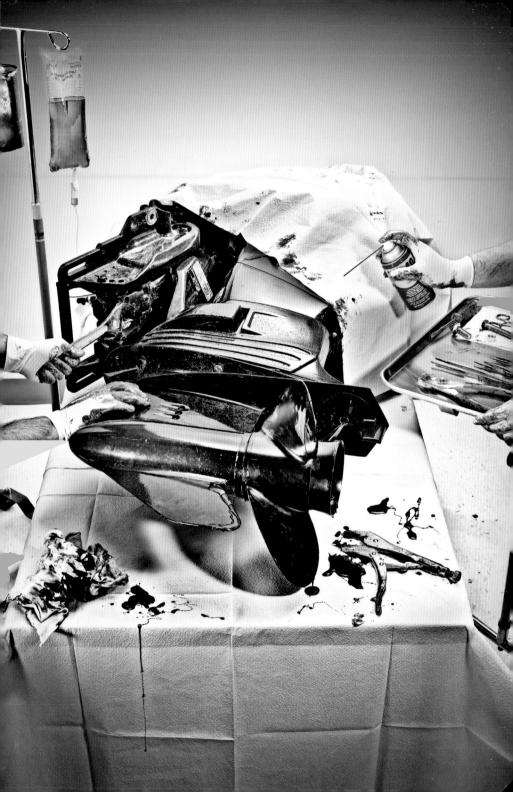

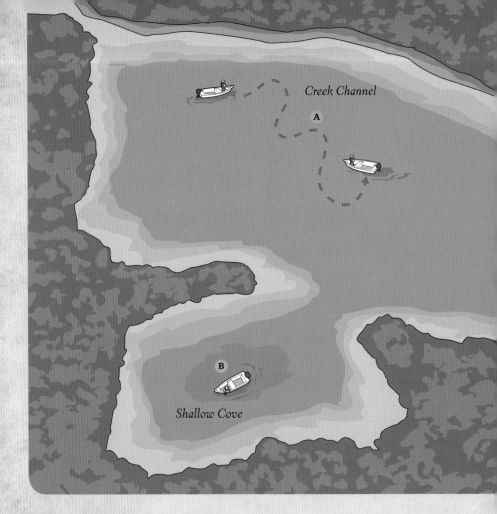

Creek Channel

A

B

Shallow Cove

23 GET UP THE CREEK

Creek channels provide some of the best action on the nation's many reservoirs. Learning to hug these structures with your boat goes a long way toward better fishing.

Start by driving at a slow to medium idle speed in a lazy "S" pattern (A) while watching your console-mounted graph for and sharp dropoffs. As you go, toss out marker buoys to delineate the edge of the dropout you plan to fish. Once you've marked a stretch with several buoys, kill

the outboard and use your trolling motor to reach the middle of the channel. Cast a diving crankbait, jig, or plastic worm perpendicular to the structure, into the adjacent shallower flat. Then work the lure back toward you, down the channel ledge, into deeper water.

If this doesn't work, reposition your boat so it's directly above the dropoff and cast parallel to it, methodically working the bait back along the channel ledge.

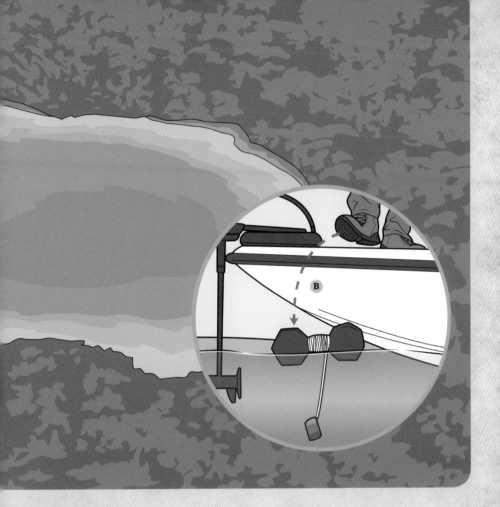

24 BE SNEAKY

Most bass are caught in less than 8 feet of water. But you'll have to get your boat into casting range—without spooking them.

RUN SILENT In the shallows, turn your outboard motor off and raise it using the power trim so the skeg doesn't drag bottom. Keep part of the skeg in the water, however, so it acts as a rudder.

GET LOW Don't just drop the trolling motor; lower it quietly. Adjust the shaft height so it doesn't hit stumps and rocks.

STAY STEADY Avoid toggling the on-off switch as you navigate. Keep the trolling motor on a slow to medium speed, and the bass will adjust to the constant noise.

MARK YOUR SPOT As you work shallow structure, such as a stump flat, keep a marker buoy near your foot. When you hook up, immediately kick the buoy into the water (B). This way, if you drift off this spot while fighting the fish, you can get right back on it—and catch more bass.

25 GIVE 'EM THE SLIP BOBBER

Slip-floats are normally used by fishermen to quickly adjust the depth at which they're fishing a live minnow to attract crappie and walleye. Using one from a belly boat, though, allows you to search for largemouths while helping you map out the lake or pond by serving as a makeshift depthfinder. First, estimate the average depth of the area you're fishing and set the float stop on your line to that length. Now fan-cast the area with a weedless, skirted jig. If the float lies on its side (A), your jig is on the bottom. If the float stands perpendicular (B), you've found deeper water. As you hop the jig back, keep an eye on the float, noting whether it's lying vertically or horizontally. By doing so, you can determine where humps, stumps, and ledges are located. If the float jerks under abruptly, then set the hook.

26 BELLY UP TO A BASS

Belly boats are cheap and offer an element of stealth that's not easily achieved in a motorized boat. Not only can you quietly enter hard-to-reach pad clusters and stick-strewn coves where big bass live, belly boat lets you present lures in new ways.

Bass boat anglers typically set up outside lily-pad clusters, tossing lures into the pads and working them back to open water. With a belly boat, you can reverse that approach to hook more fish. Kick gently to the pads (A) just far enough to get your lure into open water with a long cast. Once you're there, keep still and wait 10 to 15 minutes for the area to settle, as you may have spooked some fish.

Cast frog lures or buzzbaits into open water and retrieve into the pads. With frogs or poppers, stop the retrieve right on the edge of the vegetation for a moment or two to simulate forage trying to move into the cover. This tactic is particularly deadly early in the morning, when forage species begin moving, so get out before dawn.

27 DRAG A WORM

A belly boat's slow speed is just right for dragging a long soft-plastic worm with a curly tail. Trolling is too tiring to do all day, but you can pull a lure as you kick from spot to spot, to catch more fish and help find areas where bass are holding in deeper water.

Keep a 6- to 10-inch curly-tailed worm rigged with a wide-gap hook within reach. When you're ready to move, tie it on with no weight, make a long cast, then let out another 15 feet of line. As you kick, hold the rod low to the water. At maximum speed, the worm will gently flutter behind you in the middle of the water column (B). If you slow down, it will fall. To probe deep structure, just stop kicking and let the lure touch down (C). When you start moving again, the worm rising up off the bottom can provoke a strike.

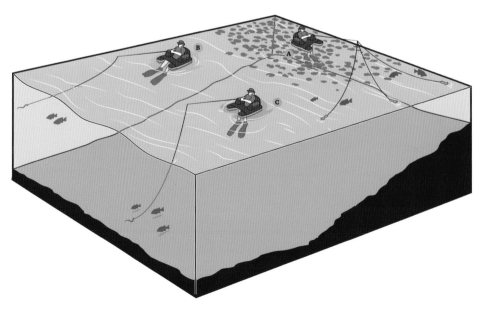

28 GET THE BASS BUGS OUT

Flyfishing for bass is a slow-paced antidote for the quick run-and-gun tactics of many conventional bass anglers. Sometimes, though, it's too relaxed. Catching bass on a surface bug is so often assumed to be a simple process that too much ends up taken for granted. Pay a little attention to these problems here, and you'll land many more bass with surface bugs.

MIND YOUR TIP One of the biggest mistakes most people make is holding the rod tip a few inches above the water. That leaves a short curve of slack line between it and the surface. When you strip a few inches of line to work the bug, the force of that strip is used up in shortening the slack and the fly moves only a little. If a bass does strike, that sag sometimes means you'll miss the fish. The rod tip should stay right on the water's surface when you're retrieving.

TURN IT OVER A poorly designed leader will fall back on itself as the final cast is completed, or it may flop to the left or right as the cast straightens. In any case, your bug will land a foot or two off target. To fix this, cut off about 18 inches from the forward end of a new 8-weight bass line so the forward taper ends more abruptly. Then use a nail knot to attach 3 feet of stiff 40-pound-test monofilament line (.025-inch diameter). Finally, attach a common 7½-foot knotless, tapered bass leader (.023-inch butt diameter) using a blood knot, and cut about a foot off the leader's 12-pound-test tippet end. The combination of stiffer butt and shorter tippet does better than most off-the-shelf leaders in turning a big bug over at the end of a cast.

DO A LITTLE SHIMMY Countless times in clear water, I've watched the gentle splat of a landing bug bring a curious bass swimming over for a look. The bug sits still. So does the bass, just hovering a few inches underneath, as if it's waiting to see what will happen next. After what seems like eternity—really only about 20 or 30 seconds—I give the bug a little twitch, just enough to wiggle its hackle and rubber legs. Most of the time, that's enough to bring a strike.

29 CATCH BASS WITHOUT A BOAT

Who says you need a fancy bass boat and a collection of expensive electronics to catch a hog? Learn to read your local pond, and you'll be able to hook up like a bass pro with your feet on the bank.

FIND THE CHANNEL There may be a small creek that enters one end of the pond itself. Try casting your buzzbait at the mouth of the creek and in a 50-foot circle in front of the mouth in the main pond. If that doesn't produce, work the channel edges with a weighted Texas-rigged plastic worm.

WORK ALL STRUCTURE Start looking for shoreline structure. The key is to spot something that looks different. A big rock, a solitary stump, a small point, and a stock fence extending into the water all potentially harbor bass. Work such spots first with a floating stickbait in short twitches and long pauses. Follow up with a slowly retrieved plastic worm.

LOOK BEFORE YOU CAST Before you walk down to the bank, watch the pond for a few minutes. You may see baitfish activity or perhaps even feeding bass. Study the shoreline for likely bass cover and decide how you'll approach it. Walk or stand in tree-shaded areas, if possible, instead of being out in the sun. This makes you less visible to fish, which also tend to lurk along shaded shorelines.

SCOUT WEEDBEDS Beds of lily pads or other weeds are obvious targets. The trick is to work a lure without hooking gobs of vegetation. Use a floating, weedless frog, which will slide over the dense mats and can be paused and twitched in small pockets of open water.

DREDGE THE DAM If the pond has a dam, the area in front of it offers both a steeply sloping underwater edge and the pond's deepest water. Texas-rigged plastic worms, lipless crankbaits, and diving stickbaits all work well parallel to the edge. Also, try dredging the deepest water with a Carolina rig, which will allow a soft-plastic worm or creature bait to hover just off the bottom as you drag it back.

FISH THROUGH SNAGS Fallen trees extending into the water attract bass. Make repetitive casts with a lightly weighted plastic worm. Work it slowly through the branches and around the trunk. Gently lift your rod tip to ease the worm over snags so you don't get hung up.

SURVEY THE CENTER Some bass will suspend at mid-depths at the center of a pond. Lipless crankbaits can be cast out to long distances and work best for reaching these fish. Experiment with retrieval speeds and allow the lure to sink to varying depths with each new cast.

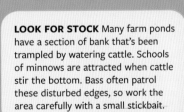

PARALLEL THE SHORELINE Don't neglect shorelines that seem featureless, such as long stretches of grassy or gravel banks. These are common to ponds without dams and can hold plenty of foraging fish. Cast parallel to shore and work a shallow-running crankbait or plastic worm slowly within a few feet of the bank.

LOOK FOR STOCK Many farm ponds have a section of bank that's been trampled by watering cattle. Schools of minnows are attracted when cattle stir the bottom. Bass often patrol these disturbed edges, so work the area carefully with a small stickbait.

30 DREDGE A BRONZEBACK

Don't get stuck in a rut of constantly feeling the need to hop a tube bait along the bottom for smallmouths, especially when the water's cold. Smallmouths can be sluggish, and are sometimes more interested in slurping up a sculpin or crayfish off the bottom than chasing a fast-moving tube up into the water column.

Next time you're fishing a lake with a soft sand or muddy bottom, try making a long cast with a tube slightly heavier than you'd normally use.

Once the tube hits the bottom, let out an extra 30 feet of line. Keep the rod tip low to the water and let the tube drag along the bottom as the boat drifts. If there's no wind, run the trolling motor slowly to create a slight drift.

As the tube bumps across the bottom, it'll kick up sand and mud like a crayfish or sculpin and the bass will take notice. When a fish eats, don't expect a hard slam, but a soft bump instead, then resistance as if you're snagged.

Green, brown, and gray tubes will work particularly well for dragging, as they most closely match the forage species that like to hang out in areas of soft bottom.

31 WAKE 'EM UP

We know guides who've landed 60-pound stripers, and a surprising number of lunker bass as well, by "waking" a large plug lure across the surface. Bass will get right in with a pack of stripers to bird-dog a baitfish school and drive it to the surface. Try using a 7½-foot baitcaster and 20-pound mono, and cast a jointed Red Fin across a tributary point, gravel bar, or hump. With the rod tip at 10 o'clock, reel just fast enough to make the

tail slosh back and forth, throwing a wake across the surface. Keep your drag loose; your next strike could be anything from a 7-pound largemouth to a 40-pound striper.

32 DO THE DOUBLE DOG

When bass begin attacking schools of baitfish in summer, target aggressive feeders with a one-two punch that combines a noisy topwater lure with a dying baitfish imitation created with a tube bait. Using two lures on a three-way swivel, this twist on the old walk-the-dog technique creates both an attention-grabbing commotion and "match-the-hatch" realism.

Look for signs of bass feeding on baitfish: swirls, shad jumping at the surface, or big schools of suspended fish on your depthfinder. Make a long

cast to your target, using a walk-the-dog retrieve to zigzag the lures across the surface. It should look like the big walking bait is chasing the little shad-imitating tube.

Bass may be reluctant to hit the noisy topwater lure, but it gets their attention. Frequently, fish that don't pound the walking bait will follow it or make a halfhearted strike. When that happens, stop your retrieve. The tube flutters down like a dying baitfish, and bass jump at it.

33 STRIKE IN THE NIGHT

Big bass lose their wariness once the lights go out, and if your lake is under pressure during the day, topwater action can be stellar after dark. The two most productive nighttime bass lures are black buzzbaits and jitterbugs, but since you won't see the strike, you can't just swing away when you hear the hit. Here's how it's done.

RESIST THE SET It's dark, so when you hear a strike, you won't know if the fish just knocked the lure or pulled it under. In spite of what your instincts will tell you, don't set. Do absolutely nothing at all for just a few seconds.

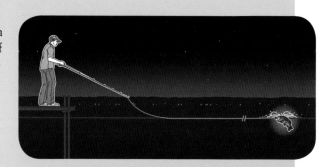

BE SURE Reel just enough to pick up any slack. Then wait for the rod to load. If the fish drops the lure and you rear back, you'll have hooks flying at your face. Make sure you feel the fish first.

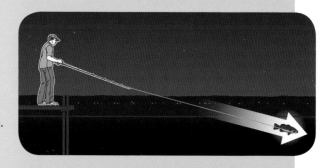

TAKE IT SLOW Sweep the rod up slowly. The bass will have had time to "walk away" with the lure and apply pressure against the line, so that there's no need to swing with all your might.

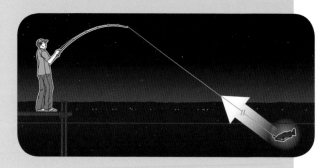

34 TUNE UP FOR SHALLOW BASS

If you're fishing for bass in a shallow, weedy lake with gear more suited to deep water, you won't have much luck. Here's how to dial in your lure arsenal for shallow-water largemouth action.

LIGHTER WORM WEIGHTS In my tests, a $^1/_{16}$-ounce weight radically outfished a $^1/_8$-ounce version, 10 fish to 1. The bass fishing world, it seems, is thinking heavier when it should be thinking lighter. Using a $^1/_{16}$- or $^1/_{32}$-ounce weight lets you tease a worm across the surface of a thick weedbed to a small pocket of open water. At that point, you can stop reeling and wait as the worm wiggles slowly downward. Its gradual sink rate allows the bass to take a good long look at your bait. A heavier weight, on the other hand, will quickly drag the worm past and below the fish, resulting in a lower strike ratio.

TAMED-DOWN TUBES Similar logic applies when it comes to soft-plastic tubes. You'll want to use jigheads designed so that the lures can be retrieved at shallow to mid-depth ranges.

NON-JIGGED JIGS So-called swimming jigs are another good example of a standard gravel-scratching lure being adapted for near-surface and mid-depth work. In their simplest form, these are your basic rubber-skirted bass jigs with the hook eye moved from the top of the jighead to the front. This configuration will mean that you can retrieve the lure straight ahead, close to the surface. Swimming jigheads also tend to be flattened on two sides, which can prevent them from hanging up amid weeds. Cast and crank them through and around weeds or other cover at a steady pace while you hold the rod at an upward angle to keep the lure moving near the surface.

35 CATCH NIGHTTIME SMALLMOUTHS

The biggest smallmouths in any lake head for the shoreline as soon as the sun sets. That's because crayfish that have been hiding all day begin to stir now, and the bass know they can grab an easy meal. Start off by mounting black lights on the sides of your boat. These purple bulbs aren't just for disco parties; they also illuminate only the first 30 to 50 feet of water and can light up your fluorescent lines without spooking the fish.

Quietly motor in on rocky banks and then flick on the black lights. Use a 14-pound fluorescent monofilament with a 4-inch crawdad in black or blue up against the bank on a Texas rig. The retrieve at night isn't any different from doing it by day, but the UV lights make everything glow in the dark. As soon as you see the line move, you set.

Some people believe that fishing at night with black lights and fluorescent line will actually make any angler a better daytime soft-plastic fisherman because the nighttime system makes

36 HUNT DOWN LARGEMOUTHS IN FALLING WATERS

In the late spring, the water levels of many lakes start to fall as the spring runoff runs its course. Bass that had moved into the normally shallow areas (to take advantage of new feeding opportunities caused by rising water levels) drop back deeper, and you are going to need to follow. Key targets are the edges of partially (or wholly) submerged brushy areas, and adjacent depths. Here's the gear and strategy you need in order to catch bass deep.

THE LURES You have two choices here— crankbaits or Carolina-rigged plastic worms. Since you want to cover water quickly to find where the bass have gone, try large-lipped crankbaits, which will dive 6 to 8 feet (some can get down to 10 to 12 feet). As for plastics, you can't go wrong with worms, but use a bullet sinker heavy enough to reach the bass.

THE TACKLE For crankbaits, experts recommend that you try a 7-foot casting outfit with a 5:1 reel ratio. A slower gear ratio lets you keep the lure in the water as long as possible. For the Carolina rig, a medium-heavy 7-foot rod works best. In this case, use a faster reel with a 7:1 ratio loaded with braided line rather than mono. This combo helps keep slack out of the line, which is vital to detecting the subtle strikes that often come with worms.

THE PRESENTATION Because the water in this springtime lake should be clearing as well as dropping, try positioning the boat a little farther out to avoid spooking fish. Your first casts should be to brush that remains partly submerged. Fish the cover thoroughly, then gradually move to deeper water until you find bass.

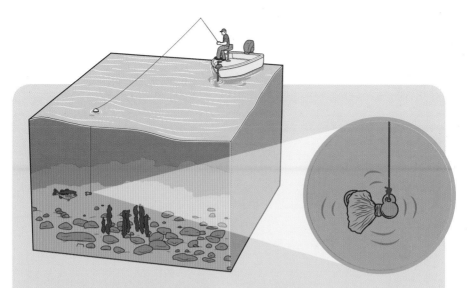

37 CATCH BASS IN THE COLD

Bass suspending in hyper-chilled water are extremely lethargic and often won't strike a moving lure. But dangling a small hair jig resembling a tiny minnow in front of their noses for a long time often gets them to open up. Put the jig 8 to 12 feet under a bobber and present it on a whippy 8-foot spinning outfit spooled with 4-pound line. Cast to a steep rock bank and let the jig sink. In choppy water, hold the rod still; waves will give the jig action. If it's calm, jiggle the rod tip slightly, pause, and repeat.

38 BACK YOUR TRAILER EASILY

Backing a boat trailer down a ramp isn't all that hard, but it does take practice. The key fact to keep in mind is that the trailer will always go in the opposite direction of the towing vehicle. This causes a great deal of confusion for newbies and it's one of the main reasons you see guys wrestling with a trailer that seems to have a mind of its own. Here's an easy way to master this maneuver:

GO SOLO Before you go anywhere near the water, practice your moves in a big, empty parking lot—the kind of place you'd go to teach a kid how to drive. Shift into reverse and then place your left hand on the bottom of the steering wheel. When you move your hand to the right (which turns the steering wheel and the front tires to the left), your trailer will move to the right (A). When you move your hand to the left—you guessed it. The wheel and front tires go right, and the trailer moves left (B).

TAKE IT SLOW Most beginners back up too fast at first. Go slowly; if the trailer starts to move in the wrong direction, stop. Pull up, straighten the trailer, and start again. Trying to correct a trailer in motion will only make matters worse. Once you master the parking lot, you're ready for the ramp.

39 CATCH BIG FISH WITH BIG LURES

By August, live-bait species have grown in size, and gamefish focus on bigger prey than whatever attracted them earlier in spring and summer. You can use larger streamer flies, spoons, lures, and live baits, and make slower retrieves. Fish in the shallows during hours when boat traffic is at a minimum and the sun is off the water. During midday, most gamefish suspend in deep water over rocky humps, sunken trees, and deeper channels.

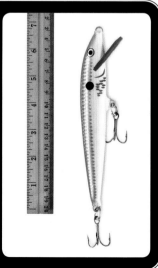

40 SCALE FISH WITH WATER

Here's an easy method for scaling fish: First, place the fish on a scaling board with its tail secured in the clamp (if you don't have a scaling board, just hold the fish down by its tail with your thumb). Next, attach an ordinary pressure nozzle to a garden hose and simply spray the scales off the fish from tail to head. Flip the fish over and do the other side. Scales come off easily with no damage to meat—and it takes less than a minute to do a whole fish!

41 FISH WITH YOUR EYES

"How in the world did you see that?" is a refrain fishing guides often hear. Learning to spot fish before you cast can dramatically increase your odds of hooking up. It doesn't require Superman vision or a carrot-rich diet to start sighting fish. Follow these rules, and you'll see your way to instant gratification on the water.

1. DISCARD DISTRACTIONS The sooner an angler can weed out any distractions like wind, ripples, and bird shadows, the sooner he can identify the position of feeding fish.

2. LOOK AHEAD Any fish that are upstream of you facing the current can't see you, so it's important to keep an eye ahead of you if you're not seeing any fish that are closer to your feet.

3. WATCH THE SURFACE The motion of schooling fish can reveal their locations. Should a noticeable disturbance occur as you stare at a smooth water surface, keep looking. Flashes of tails often follow in spots where you first see ripples.

4. ZERO IN Instead of searching the entire area, focus on one small zone at a time. Tunnel vision can actually be a good thing whenever you're contemplating where to place that next cast.

5. SPOT INCONSISTENCIES Whether you're seeking out bedded bass or trout holding in a run, try to identify unusual marks in the water. Color shades, shadows, and motion can tip you off to a lurking fish.

6. GET THE EYES Polarized-lens sunglasses are a must. You can't see fish without them. Try to position yourself so that the sun makes a spotlight on the water, and wear the right color lenses for the conditions.

7. LOOK THROUGH Practice looking through the water column—not fixing your gaze on the surface or the bottom. Doing this lets you observe motion and subtle color changes that pinpoint fish.

8. SEARCH FOR THE SUBTLE Look for reflections, shapes, and shadows that might reveal a fish. A tail or a nose can be all you need to identify a target.

42 GO DARK AND DEEP

When smallmouths scatter along rocks and weeds in their post-spawn funk, try turning to the seductive synergy of a jig-and-crawler combination. You can fish deep and cover a lot of territory, and the crawler seems to be the perfect touch for this transitional time, when the smallmouths have yet to lock on to a preferred forage. Dark jigs—black, brown, and purple—seem to match a nightcrawler's color. Try using a whole crawler and jig with a marabou feather skirt. When you feel a hit, drop the rod for a few seconds before setting.

43

MAKE A DOUBLE-SIDED WORM CAN

Instead of digging down into the bottom of a coffee can to find your worms, replace the metal end of the can with another plastic lid in which you've punched a dozen tiny little airholes. When the worms burrow down to the bottom, simply turn the can over and open the other end.

44 GET THE DROP ON BASS

If it's done right, a drop-shot rig can be irresistible to even picky fish. The key is the rate at which it sinks; soft-plastic bait should fall flat through the water, instead of diving nose-down. To accomplish this, try a $\frac{1}{32}$-ounce split shot. During the spawn and postspawn, shorten the space between the bait and the tag end, where you hang the split shot, to about 4 inches or less (A). By cutting the tag end down, you minimize the problem of tangling around structures. Bass will often attack the soft plastic as it falls down through the water. If the bait hits bottom without a strike, shake the rod to give the worm some enticing action. After a few shakes, gently retrieve the bait and then cast to your next target.

Concentrate on tempting shallow-water largemouths around docks, near deadfall, and adjacent to vegetation (B). Also, try to

intercept postspawn lunkers on shelves adjacent to flats (C).

Try fishing a 7-foot medium-action spinning rod and a spinning reel spooled with green fluorocarbon line. In open water, you'll want to use 6-pound line; near structure, use an 8- to 10-pound line. For the rig, use a 7-inch worm in triple margarita, a 4/0 Gamakatsu EWG hook, and one $\frac{1}{32}$-ounce split shot. Work at close

range, pitching around tree limbs, docks, and so forth.

Because this rig requires a light line, target a spot close to where you think bass are and entice them away from cover. The natural action of the gliding drop-shot bait will make this possible.

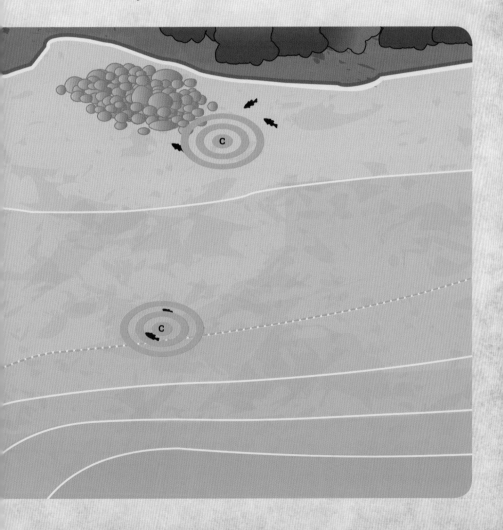

45 CATCH SMALLMOUTHS WITH THE BAIT THAT BITES BACK

There's really nothing new about hellgrammites. These giant aquatic larvae are still expensive. Their pincers still draw blood. But anglers will gladly put up with all of that because, when it comes to hellgrammites, they still catch more moving-water smallmouths than any other bait today. Anglers who put serious stock in 'mites can save cash by seining their own in late spring and summer using a good piece of door screening stretched between two posts. One angler lifts rocks, while the other stands downstream with the makeshift seine to collect hellgrammites that flush downcurrent. Once you have your bait, you can make it last awhile with proper hooking. Slide the point of a longshank hook just once under the collar, which is the first body segment behind the head. Hellgrammites are hardy, and hooked this way, the bait should slide right up the line when a bass attacks, allowing you to reseat the hellgrammite and cast out again.

46 SHAKE THE BED FOR GIANT BASS

The first big breeders will spawn in bays, coves, and boat canals. With polarized sunglasses on, look near flooded bushes, boat docks, blowdowns, and grass edges. Any of these could hide a giant bass. Keep searching until you find one. Remember, it often takes big bait to rouse a bedded superbass; try a lifelike swimbait, to mimic a bream feeding on bass eggs. Cast beyond the bass and then swim the lure into the bed, working it there until you find a spot to aggravate the fish. Twitch your rod tip on a slack line to make the bait bounce up and down like a feeding bluegill. Hold on tight!

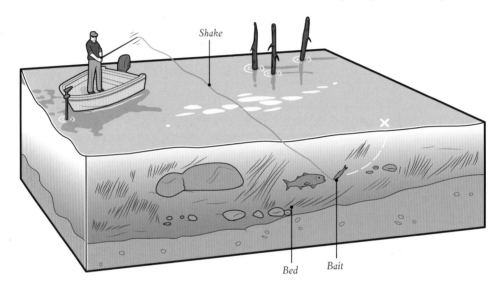

Shake

Bed *Bait*

47 SEND JERKBAITS DOWN DEEP

Big prespawn bass of all sizes stack up on main-lake points at the mouths of spawning bays, as well as secondary points within them. These are often the last stops bass make before they hit the shallows to breed. The key here is to bypass those smaller fish available within 3 feet of the surface, specifically targeting bigger females below, in 5 to 8 feet of water.

A long-billed, suspending jerkbait in clown color gets down to where these monsters hold. Cast over the point and make the jerkbait dive quickly with just two or three sideways pulls. Then let it suspend. To tempt the biggest bass, the secret is to keep the bait still for up to 30 seconds, twitch it once, and rest it again. Patience pays off in impressive dividends here.

48 RIP A RATTLEBAIT

The rule of thumb for prespawn cold-water bass is to fish slow. But like every other rule, this one is made to be broken, which you can do with a lipless rattling crankbait. Concentrate on the points and submerged grassbeds, as well as 45-degree banks and flats adjacent to creek-channel bends. In the early-season period, try out crayfish patterns, particularly those that are bright orange-and-red in stained water and green-and-brown in clear water. With 8-pound monofilament, you can run an unmodified lure down about 7 feet. Instead of using a deliberate stop-and-go retrieve, which is emplyed by many anglers now, try keeping the nose of your bait quickly tapdancing over the bottom. This faster retrieve covers more water, increasing the odds of running the rattler through the strike zone of a bass. In the cold water, the fish's strike zone is going to be significantly smaller. If you get the lure in its face, the bass is going to bite.

49 TIE A PALOMAR KNOT

STEP 1 Extend about 6 inches of doubled line through the eye of the hook or lure.

STEP 2 Tie a loose overhand knot using the doubled line on either side of the eye. The hook itself will hang from the middle of the knot.

STEP 3 Pass the loop over the hook. Wet the knot with saliva and then pull on the doubled line (but not the loop) to tighten. Trim closely.

This is the most widely useful—and the easiest—of all terminal knots used in freshwater and inshore saltwater fishing. It works well with both nylon monofilaments and superbraids.

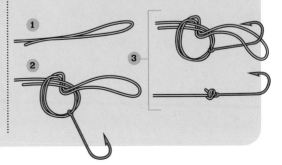

50

PULL BASS FROM BENEATH THE BOARDS

Bass like docks because they provide shelter and a steady supply of bluegills, shad, and other baitfish. But how the largemouths relate to docks in spring depends on the spawning stage. This time of year, on any given lake, you'll find bass in all three modes: prespawn, spawn, and postspawn. Here's how to fish near docks, no matter which stage the fish are in.

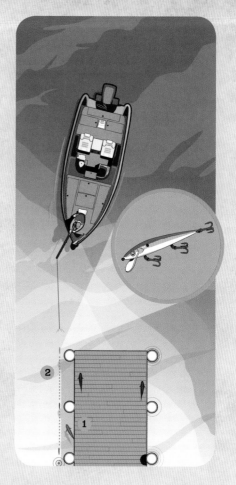

PRESPAWN Concentrate on docks near spawning areas where there is quick access to deeper water, such as those near main-lake points, secondary points, and steep banks. Work a shad-colored suspending jerkbait parallel to the outer edges of the docks, where prespawn bass tend to hold (1). Let the bait hover for 3 seconds or more between twitches (2). Another excellent choice is a $^1/4$- to $^1/2$-ounce black-and-blue skirted jig matched with a pork-rind trailer. Swim it a few feet beneath the surface along the dock's edges to imitate a bluegill. Or hop it along the bottom to mimic a crayfish.

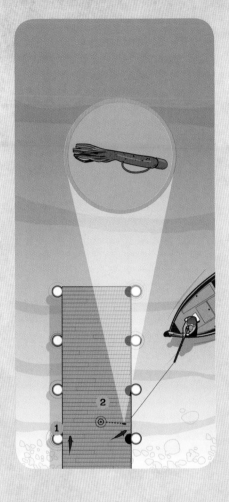

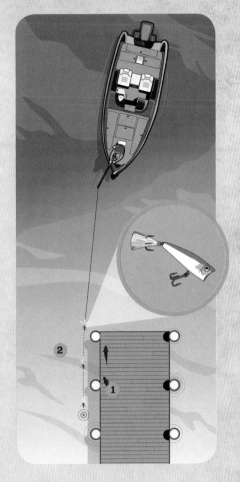

SPAWN Spawning bass will gravitate to docks in shallow water, typically toward the pilings at the nearshore end (1). They also frequently spawn directly underneath the walkway connecting floating docks to shore. Give a 4- or 4^1/2-inch Texas-rigged tube a try here, pegging a ^{3}/16- to ^{5}/16-ounce bullet sinker against the lure to keep it from sliding up the line. Flipping, pitching, or skipping the lure far under the dock will produce the most strikes (2). Although it takes time to master the flip, the cleaner the presentation, the more strikes you'll draw, as the first drop often counts most.

POSTSPAWN When the spawning period wanes, you can still find excellent topwater action around docks. Before heading back toward deep water, postspawn bass may continue to hold near shallow docks for a few days. They tend to suspend under a dock's outside edges (1) and will nail a topwater popper worked past them (2). The window of opportunity can be relatively short for postspawn stragglers, since their willingness to stay will depend largely on the amount of forage species around the dock. However, these bass can offer some of the most exciting fishing of the year.

51 SHAKE YOUR HEAD

Why reinvent the jig? Because a few tweaks can start a craze that anglers swear catches more and bigger bass. Lengthen the shank to accommodate weedless rigging, turn the line-tie eye 90 degrees and move it forward, and you've got a basic shaky-head jig. The design allows a floating soft-plastic worm or crawfish to stand perpendicular to the bottom, where subtle rod shakes get it wiggling in place. The tactic isn't new; it's just never had a name before. It does now: shaky-head fishing

52 LEARN TO SWIM

When largemouths are done with spawning they stack up near flooded bushes in coves and in grassbeds on tributary points. And so, it's time to swim—your baits, that is. The bass will key in on active forage, especially small bluegills, and a swimming presentation with a jig, creature bait, or lizard can be a fast way to add some serious weight to your stringer.

TACKLE When the sun is high, target the shade around flooded bushes with a 6½-foot medium-heavy spinning rod and some 10-pound monofilament. For fishing into grassbeds, go with a 7-foot medium-heavy baitcasting outfit with 20-pound line; this will help you haul out bass that have buried themselves in the weeds when hooked.

LURES Top lures for swimming include a watermelon, white, or black lizard; creature bait also in black or watermelon; or a ¼- to ½-ounce black-and-blue jig. Rig both the lizard and creature Texas-style with a ³⁄₁₆- to ¼-ounce tungsten sinker and an extra-wide-gap hook and add a V-chunk or grub trailer to the jig.

TECHNIQUE Cast into grassbeds or pitch your lure underhand to get beneath flooded bushes. Engage your reel before your bait sinks all the way to the bottom, lift the rod to about 11 o'clock, and retrieve steadily—fast enough to keep the lure off the bottom or above the grass. It's critical to determine what type of retrieve the fish want. Keep the rod rock-steady and adjust the retrieve speed with the reel. If this fails, you can try twitching the rod tip while you continue to reel. The most important thing to remember is that unlike most retrieves with a jig or soft-plastic bait, in this case you want to keep that bait moving.

53 SKIP A JIG IN TIGHT QUARTERS

Underneath docks and overhanging trees are likely spots to find unpressured, hard-to-reach bass. Introduce those bass to your lure with this skipping trick.

Holding the rod sidearm, start your cast with the rod pointed at the water (not at your target). Moving to the left (right if you're a lefty), rotate your arms and the rod above your head and back down your right side. You're making a complete, vertical circle with the rod and accelerating as you complete the cast. Finish with the rod tip pointed directly at your target as the line shoots off the reel. So, if you're aiming at a spot tucked behind two dock posts, your eyes and your rod tip should be pointed right between the posts as you accelerate and stop the cast. It's harder to skip at short

range than at a distance of 30 feet, where momentum works in your favor. Try not to overpower the cast. Accuracy and distance, as in skipping stones, are all about angles— and that comes with practice.

Focus on shady spots that are tight to the bank. Overhanging limbs are good target zones, but beneath docks is best. Look for signs of recent spawning activity in the near vicinity—barren patches of sand and gravel in water 4 feet deep or shallower. Then, concentrate your casts in areas from the edge of the dock to bulkheads or shoreline. Try a medium-heavy rod with a baitcast reel and 17- to 20-pound fluorocarbon line. For a lure, try using a ³⁄₈-ounce jig in green pumpkin, brown, or black. Modify jigs for "skipping season" by trimming the skirt.

54

KNOW YOUR:
SMALLMOUTH BASS

Much like largemouths, smallmouth bass can be fooled into eating anything from live bait to flies to just about every style of artificial lure available. The big thing that sets them apart, however, is their scrappy nature. Smallmouths are known for the bulldog fighting abilities that trump their largemouth cousins. Hook a smallmouth in a deep lake, and it's going to make every effort to swim to the bottom and snap your line. Hook one in a swift, rocky river, and it will do its best to find a boulder to wrap around and break you off. Although these fish can be found throughout the United States in many types of water, the habitat that they prefer includes a combination of cooler waters, rocky structure, and current, making them much more prevalent in rivers than largemouth bass, particularly in the Northeast and Northwest.

55

USE MONSTER TUBES IN THE SHALLOWS

Once they begin spawning, the trick to catching giant bass is spotting them on or near their beds. Wear polarized sunglasses and slowly cruise the sheltered shallows, looking for any nests on firm beds such as sand or gravel—especially along sunny banks and near stumps, docks, windfalls, or other cover.

Go with a 6-inch tube in pearl, rigged Texas-style with a 6/0 worm hook and ¼-ounce bullet sinker. This oversized tube rouses extra-large fish. Slip into casting range of the bed, and when that big female faces away, pitch the tube softly into her nest, using a stout flipping rod matched with some 20-pound fluorocarbon line. Lightly twitch the bait in place. Experiment until you find a good action that will aggravate the bass. Then keep it up until she inhales it.

56 HAVE A BIG BASS AFTER-PARTY

Postspawn largemouth fishing doesn't have to be slow. Yes, some of the bass are briefly more focused on resting than feeding. But they'll cream a bait if you put it in front of them. And after a short recovery period, largemouths go on a major feeding binge. Here are a few ways to take advantage of that gluttony.

WHACK THE WILLOWS Early on in the morning, whack the willows with a boat oar. Newly hatched mayflies will be clinging to the bushes in droves, and they'll drop to the surface, thus drawing hungry baitfish. In just a few hours, big bass lured by the sounds of fish feeding on the surface will move in, too. Cast a popper tight to the bushes and retrieve it aggressively so it spits and pops. Lunkers will love it.

WORM THE BANK Many bass tuck themselves up against shallow, shaded banks after spawning to take a breather for a day or two. They won't be feeding heavily yet, but you can still provoke bite after bite with a worm that's Texas-rigged weightless on a 3/0 offset hook. Go with a hot color like Merthiolate orange or bubblegum pink.

CRANK THE WEEDS Weedlines are major stopovers for bass heading for deeper water in natural lakes. Set up near the edge of the weedline and cast a gold or silver lipless crankbait parallel to the cover. Then burn it on back to trigger savage strikes.

TWITCH THE POINT In reservoirs, primary points that form the mouths of tributary arms are the final stop before postspawn bass venture into the main lake. They're seriously hungry now and have come to the right place: Massive schools of threadfin shad feeding on drifting plankton blooms periodically pass this point. Fling a ½-ounce spook-style topwater lure in a roadkill pattern past the breaking fish. Then retrieve it with quick twitches of the rod tip and hang on tight.

57 KEEP ON THE GRASS

Although smallmouth bass often hang out near rocks and gravel, they'll also feel right at home in aquatic vegetation, especially right after the spawn, when smallies head to prey-rich weedbeds to fatten up before they migrate to their summer haunts. Look for productive greenery on points, humps, and on the edges of dropoffs in 3 to 8 feet of water (or a little deeper in clear lakes). The bass will relate to the outside edges of the weeds, as well as all the lanes and pockets that make ideal ambush zones. Use any of these tactics to pluck bass from the grass.

DANCE A TOPWATER BAIT This is a proven winner for this kind of fishing. Make long casts with a 7-foot medium-heavy baitcasting rod, a high-speed reel, and 15-pound line.

Work that popper or spook all the way back to the boat, and then steel yourself for some explosive strikes.

BURN A SPINNERBAIT You can trigger jolting reflex strikes by sending one over the grass. Use the same kind of casting outfit as above, tying on a ½- to ¾-ounce chartreuse spinnerbait rigged with slightly undersize double-willow chartreuse blades, which will keep the bait from rolling.

SWIM A TUBE Slide a 1/16-ounce jig with exposed hook into a 3½-inch root beer–green flake tube, and tie it onto a 10-pound line with a 6½-foot medium-heavy spinning setup. Cast it out and work the bait in very slowly. If it's done right, the lure will almost seem to hover over the grass and coax bites even from tentative bass.

58 GO ON THE OFFSHORE OFFENSIVE

After spawning, big largemouths and smallmouths gravitate toward deeper structures, where they lie in wait for passing baitfish schools. Armed with a fishfinder and a set of marker buoys, you can tap into some hot bass action in these offshore honey holes.

SUBMERGED HUMPS Bass loiter around the edges of these structures, feeding when shad schools approach. Fan cast a topwater lure around the hump and dog-walk it back to your boat for an explosive surface strike.

RESERVOIR POINTS The fishiest points tend to extend a long distance away from shore with a gradual taper, eventually cascading into a deep river channel. Bass will hunker down next to isolated stumps and rocks on the tops and ends of these structures.

LEDGES These flat-topped feeding shelves drop quickly into deep water. Largemouths gather here in summer and can be caught by dragging a ½ - to ¾-ounce football jig with a trailer around cover near the breakline.

59 TAKE IT TO THE SLOPES

Steep structures allow sluggish early-spring bass to make major depth changes without swimming long distances. It's just a simple matter of conserving energy. A bass on a main-lake flat, for example, might have to swim 200 yards or more to go from 3 to 12 feet of water, but on a vertical rock bluff that fish can reach the same depths by swimming only 9 feet.

ROCK BLUFFS These structures will consistently produce prespawn bass, and because the rock walls are typically fairly apparent above the shoreline, they're easy to locate. Look for bass to suspend along the face of bluffs, where they'll make quick vertical movements to pick off baitfish.

STANDING TIMBER In spring, target emergent timber that lines the edges of major creek runs, rather than submerged timber along very deep river channels. Bass will suspend around the trees, warming themselves in the sun, and then move into the shade to ambush prey.

SUBMERGED HUMPS Avoid the tops of these structures in spring. Instead, use your graph to pinpoint the side or end with the sharpest slope. That's where the biggest bass will hang out. Then drop a jig or a drop-shot-rigged worm almost straight down to the fish.

RETAINING WALLS In lakes that have a good deal of residential development on or around them, the banks are often lined in wood pilings or concrete blocks to prevent erosion. Bass readily cruise these vertical walls looking for shad and crayfish. When they're not feeding, they'll drop back and suspend off the structure.

45-DEGREE BANKS Technically, these banks are far from vertical, but they slope into deep water fairly quickly and they often have small, steep ledges on them that hold bass. A suspending jerkbait will work here and in all of these places if the water is clear; fish it with slow twitches.

60 JIG A WORM

Tournament pros like a plastic worm on a jighead—but not just any worm or jighead. The worm, 4 to 6 inches, must be very skinny. The round-ball jighead usually weighs $^1/8$ to $^1/4$ ounce and has a size 1/0 hook. This setup is used with 8-pound-test line in shallow or deep water, depending on the cover. Let it sink but keep it off the bottom. Once the lure is in the zone, give it a shake, and the skinny worm will respond

with a shimmy. Effective depths can range from 10 to 30 feet at places such as deep points, bluffs, and boathouses.

61 CAST THE CRANKS OF SPRING

When it comes to hooking coldwater bass in early spring, crankbaits can't be beat. These lures swim with a tight wiggle that appeals to lethargic bass in water below 50 degrees. Here are four varieties to keep in your tackle box.

COFFIN BILLS A crankbait with a coffin bill fends off snags. A $^1/_2$-ounce lure is heavy enough to cast accurately to windfalls and other snaggy cover. Crank slowly as it comes through the structure, and pause every time it pops over a limb.

LIPLESS RATTLERS The majority of this type of sinking, hard-vibrating crank-bait have noisy rattles. Slow-roll yours over submerged grass 5 to 10 feet deep. Most strikes are going to happen after you snap the rattler through a strand of the grass.

FLAT DIVERS These will descend to 8 feet and have nearly neutral buoyancy. They're ideal for cranking banks that slope into the water at a 45-degree angle. Target the pea gravel to basketball-size chunk rock at the mouths of spawning coves. Tick the bottom with a slow to medium-slow retrieve. Go with a shad or crawfish color.

THIN MINNOWS The subtle roll and twitch tempts bites when sluggish bass shun more active lures. Try running it over 45-degree-angle banks and secondary points. Or slowly retrieve the lure parallel to each side of a dock to pull bass from beneath. Giving it an occasional stop-and-go cadence can make a huge difference.

62 LEARN DEEP SECRETS

Two places where you can consistently find active bass when it's hot out are the long, sloping points that reach far offshore before dropping off and the lips of creek and river channels, called ledges, especially on outside bends and channel junctures.

Start by idling around the main lake while viewing your depthfinder. Normally, you'll see suspended fish, which are typically inactive at a certain depth, often about 14 feet or so. Remember that number once you determine it, because that's where you're going to find feeding bass on points and ledges throughout the lake.

DEEP CRANKING Comb the points and ledges with a $^1/_2$- to 1-ounce, long-billed, shad-pattern crankbait that will run deep enough to tap the bottom at the depth that you're fishing. Use a 7-foot medium-action baitcasting rod and 8-pound line, and make long casts to get your bait to its maximum depth. These crankbaits will work best at 18 feet or shallower.

CAROLINA RIGGING For fishing waters down to 30 feet or more, it's hard to beat a Carolina rig, which casts far, sinks fast, and stays in the strike zone throughout the retrieve. Cast these with a heavy-action 7- to $7^1/_2$-foot baitcasting outfit. Use a 4-inch french-fry worm Texas-rigged on a 3/0 worm hook. Watermelon and pumpkinseed are proven summertime colors.

HEAVY JIGGING If you're after big bass in particular, cast a $^1/_2$- to $3/_4$-ounce weedless jig dressed with a plastic craw, using a 7-foot medium-heavy baitcasting rod and 12-pound line. Go with crawdad colors in clear water and black-and-blue in stained water. After casting, jump the jig off the bottom with long sweeps of the rod and then let it swing back to the bottom while you hold the rod tip high. This bait isn't apt to catch as many fish as the subtler Carolina rig, but the jig's big profile will trigger strikes from some of the lake's heftiest bass.

63 FIND LATE-SUMMER LARGEMOUTHS

By late summer, bass fishing is not for the faint of heart. Largemouths are often deep and lethargic, and they're also frequently starting to relocate and suspend at mid-depth ranges as forage begins to move. This is when the professional anglers start following the ABCs of summer fishing: aquatic vegetation, bridges, and current, the three shortcuts to finding fish.

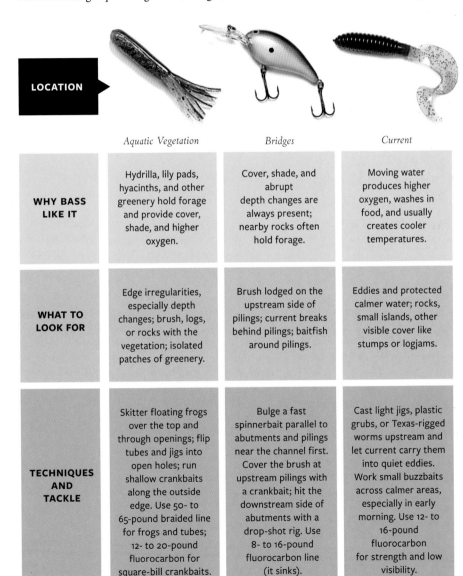

LOCATION	*Aquatic Vegetation*	*Bridges*	*Current*
WHY BASS LIKE IT	Hydrilla, lily pads, hyacinths, and other greenery hold forage and provide cover, shade, and higher oxygen.	Cover, shade, and abrupt depth changes are always present; nearby rocks often hold forage.	Moving water produces higher oxygen, washes in food, and usually creates cooler temperatures.
WHAT TO LOOK FOR	Edge irregularities, especially depth changes; brush, logs, or rocks with the vegetation; isolated patches of greenery.	Brush lodged on the upstream side of pilings; current breaks behind pilings; baitfish around pilings.	Eddies and protected calmer water; rocks, small islands, other visible cover like stumps or logjams.
TECHNIQUES AND TACKLE	Skitter floating frogs over the top and through openings; flip tubes and jigs into open holes; run shallow crankbaits along the outside edge. Use 50- to 65-pound braided line for frogs and tubes; 12- to 20-pound fluorocarbon for square-bill crankbaits.	Bulge a fast spinnerbait parallel to abutments and pilings near the channel first. Cover the brush at upstream pilings with a crankbait; hit the downstream side of abutments with a drop-shot rig. Use 8- to 16-pound fluorocarbon line (it sinks).	Cast light jigs, plastic grubs, or Texas-rigged worms upstream and let current carry them into quiet eddies. Work small buzzbaits across calmer areas, especially in early morning. Use 12- to 16-pound fluorocarbon for strength and low visibility.

64 ADJUST THE CONTRAST

In the summer, bass pros say, you have a much better chance at a true hog of a largemouth after dark. Boat traffic in the day makes a whole lot of noise in the water, and it's tougher for bass to pick up on the sound of natural bait. They might strike lures during the day because they're confused by all the engine noise, which is all very well and good, but once they make mistakes during the day a few times, they'll just stop feeding when it's light.

Instead, wary bass go on the hunt when the water quiets down at night. To catch them, patrol flats with quick access to deeper water, where the fish will move in to feed. Use a ¾-ounce short-arm spinner-bait with a single Colorado blade. The heavy lure sinks quickly, which is key to using a pump-and-stop retrieve that lets you mimic a crayfish hopping along the bottom. At night, pros know that contrast is more important than color. Use a black or purple spinnerbait with a white pork-chunk trailer. The trailer creates a slight difference in contrast on the bottom. Big bass will usually hit anything that's moving the right way and stands out a little against the background.

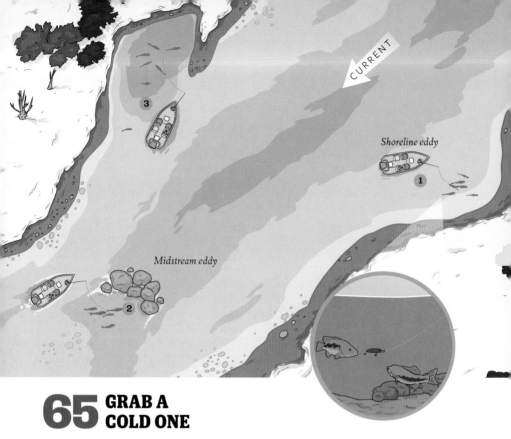

Shoreline eddy

Midstream eddy

CURRENT

65 GRAB A COLD ONE

Though smallmouth bass may be harder to hook in moving winter water, there are still bigger fish for the catching from December through February. Small bass eat very small forage in winter; big fish may not feed often, but they'll look for larger food that provides lots of energy. Success comes from tracking the weather, using the sun, and finding ideal bottom structure. Here are some top pro secrets to get you started.

1. SAND TRAP Anywhere that there's a transition from hard to soft bottom is a great place to start. Baitfish prefer a soft bottom— something the smallies know. Look out for sandy 7- to 10-foot-deep eddies on west-facing banks because they get the most sun. You can hook on a diving twitchbait such as an XCalibur Xt3 worked super-slowly with long pauses. West-facing banks receive the

most sun, so hit them at the warmest point in the day. You might find a few fish there, searching for food wherever hard bottom meets soft.

2. PET ROCKS Target slack rock eddies with soft bottoms during slight warming trends. With their metabolism slowed, fish lurking there won't dart into the current to eat. But barely twitch a soft-plastic tube in the calm eddy head and you can pick off one or two.

3. HOLE PUNCH If all else fails, find a 15- to 20-foot-deep slack hole and have at it, though this is a hard place to catch fish. Uses rabbit- or fox-hair jigs, as the material pulses even when the jig sits motionless on the bottom. Keep the jig still, imparting the slightest occasional twitch.

66 GO SPINNERBAITING FOR COLDWATER BASS

You can catch big wintertime bass by slow-rolling a spinnerbait in water as cold as 47 degrees Fahrenheit. After a sunny warm front has been baking the surface water for a few days, bass come up out of deeper water in a feeding mode. Carefully casting to fallen trees is the key. You'll be able to pluck winter bass from main-lake windfalls on steep, rocky banks. Here, the bass can quickly move shallow or deep in response to the weather. When they swim up after a warm front, they typically suspend in the outer limbs of fallen trees. They'll readily nab a spinnerbait swimming above them.

THE TACKLE In most situations, you'll do best by slinging spinnerbaits with a 7-foot medium-heavy baitcasting rod matched to 50-pound braided line (A). The exception is in crystal-clear water, where pros suggest

14-pound fluorocarbon. Braided line is so sensitive that you'll know instantly when you bump a limb or get a strike. The bites can be light when the water's cold.

THE LURE A ¾-ounce chartreuse-and-white Booyah spinnerbait (B) is a winter workhorse. Try a small nickel Colorado blade ahead of a gold No. 7 willowleaf blade. The big willowleaf lets you crawl the spinnerbait at the slow speeds that appeal to sluggish bass hanging 5 to 12 feet deep.

THE TECHNIQUE Slow-roll a spinnerbait across the limbs at a 45-degree angle (C). Let the bait sink to the depth you want to fish before you start retrieving. If the bass are less than 5 feet deep, switch over to a ½-ounce spinnerbait.

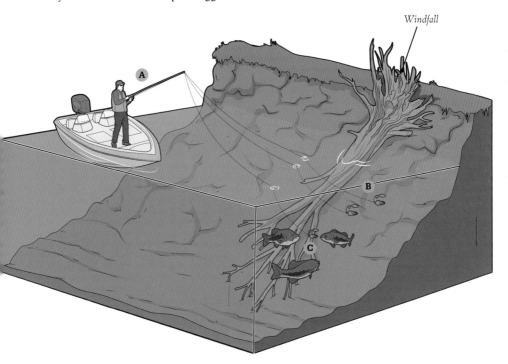

Windfall

67 CRANK POCKETS FOR PRESPAWN BASS

With water temperatures approaching 48 degrees in early spring, largemouth bass in murky reservoirs vacate their deep winter haunts and move into shallow indentations or "pockets" that are found along tributary shorelines, holding there around submerged stumps and logs. This pattern is strongest on calm, clear, sunny days when a smartly worked crankbait will draw strikes.

THE TACKLE Accuracy and winching power trump long-distance casting capability. A sensitive 6½-foot baitcaster capable of handling lines to 20-pound-test is perfect for this application. Pair it with a baitcasting reel spooled with abrasion-resistant 17-pound monofilament.

THE LURE Go with a shallow-running, square-bill crankbait with a short, blunt diving lip. It's a buoyant lure designed for banging off wood cover with a minimum of hangups. Color schemes like firetiger, shad, and crayfish score well in early spring.

THE TARGET Work shallow pockets with scattered stumps, logs, and blowdowns in murky reservoir tributary arms. Bass hold tight to wood on sunny days (A) but roam farther from the cover under cloudy skies. Start in the upper end of the creek arm, where the water is likely to be warmest and murkiest, and then gradually fish out into the main lake.

THE PRESENTATION Cast just beyond your target and begin reeling slowly and steadily, using the rod to steer the lure directly into the cover. In this "crash-and-burn" kind of cranking, you want the lure steamrollered right into the wood (B). Don't be afraid of hanging up.

68 TAKE SWIMMING LESSONS

In early springtime, bass move onto reservoir flats to warm up prior to spawning. They're sluggish in cold water, so they'll often ignore a fast-moving crankbait or bulky spinnerbait. But a jig that is swimming like a slow-moving baitfish is an offer they often can't refuse. A weedless jig between ⅛- and ⅜-ounce, in black, brown, or green pumpkin works best with this horizontal presentation. Tip the hook with a matching pork- or plastic-chunk trailer to add some realistic fluttering action. Fish this combo on a 7-foot medium-heavy spinning or baitcasting outfit using 8- to 12-pound-test fluorocarbon line.

STEP 1 Position your boat on the outer edge of the flat, ideally in 10 to 12 feet of water. Bass will hold around bottom transitions—areas where gravel changes to mud or mud changes to chunk rock—and scattered wood or rock cover. Make a long cast and let the jig sink to the bottom.

STEP 2 With your rod held rock-steady at two o'clock, reel quickly so the jig shoots off the bottom, and then begin a medium-slow steady retrieve so it swims like a baitfish. The trick is to retrieve the jig so it follows the bottom contour. If you feel it drag bottom, reel a little faster. If you haven't felt it drag in a while, slow down a little until it does; then speed up again.

STEP 3 Bass strikes are often light in cold water. If you feel a tick or if you can detect any suspicious weight on your line, set the hook hard.

69 COVER THE COVER

Largemouths will charge spinnerbaits from any type of cover, but they tend to prefer various areas on any given day. Find out where the bass are currently holding, and then focus your efforts accordingly. You'll need to probe shallow grassbeds, boat docks, stumps, flooded bushes, the limbs of fallen trees, and any other available cover until the bass tell you where to fish for them.

Take advantage of your lure's characteristics when searching for these bass. The spinnerbait is one of the most snag-resistant lures and efficiently combs vast amounts of water (even at low speeds). Cast beyond the cover when possible and then guide your spinnerbait close to it with your rod tip. Don't overlook the riprap and rocky banks; bass often position themselves nearby in shallow water when it's raining. Move your boat close to the bank, cast parallel to the shoreline, and keep your bait hard to the rocks throughout the retrieve. When a bass takes a shot, you'll know, because it won't be subtle.

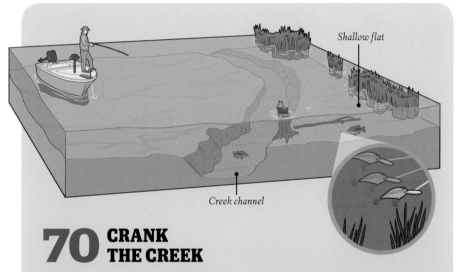

Shallow flat

Creek channel

70 CRANK THE CREEK

As the prespawn progresses and smaller male bass begin cruising the skinniest nearshore waters, the biggest females lurk nearby. But they tend to remain hidden, gravitating toward any slightly deeper water within flats and bays. This makes any reservoir creek channels and ditches—which may bottom out at only 3 or 4 feet—the hottest mega-bass spots just prior to the spawn.

The tight wiggling produced by a flat-sided crankbait really triggers these fish to bite. Launch your crankbait across a creek channel or ditch and run it at medium speed over the edge of a drop. Keep the lure bumping the bottom and bouncing off any cover. In clear water, retrieve a jerkbait over the wood. Pay special attention to tree stumps and logs along the edge.

71 GO SLINGIN' IN THE RAIN

A spinnerbait is my first choice for wet springtime bass fishing. Rain usually means a falling barometer, which makes bass more inclined to feed and chase. The darker skies and dimpled surface reduce light penetration and encourage bass to move to the edges of their cover, for a much-enlarged strike zone. You don't have to put your bait within inches of a bass's nose to prompt a bite. Merely get it close enough for the fish to see it or sense the vibration through its lateral lines. A bass in a rainy-day mode won't overlook a flashing, pulsating spinner-bait. To fish shallow water in a steady rain, I like to use a light-colored lure, usually one like a white $\frac{3}{8}$- or $\frac{1}{2}$-ounce spinnerbait with nickel blades. I opt for rounded Indiana or Colorado blades, which have more lift, when I want to run the lure slowly just beneath the surface. If I need to retrieve the bait a little faster or deeper, I switch over to narrower willowleaf blades. Heavy 15- to 20-pound-test line can help reduce break-offs in thick cover. When the rain breaks or turns to showers, I downsize. A big spinnerbait fished in slick water may look too gaudy to bass. I've had success going as small as $\frac{1}{8}$ ounce, in white, with a No. 2 Indiana and a No. 3 Colorado or Oklahoma blade. If you can't find a small spinnerbait in one of these combinations, buy one that has a Colorado lead blade and a willowleaf trailing, and replace the latter with another Colorado blade. I fish with these diminutive versions just as I do the larger ones, and with the same heavy line—and I still draw strikes from some sizable bass.

MOUNT YOUR CATCH AND EAT IT, TOO

Ever notice that you can gauge the size of a fish just by looking at the tail? If you don't want to pay for a replica mount or waste the meat by having a skin mount made, fillet your next whopper, save the tail, and make your own trophy.

STEP 1 Remove as much meat as possible from the base of the tail with a sharp knife or grapefruit spoon. With wire cutters, clip the spine as far back as possible. Don't damage the skin or lose any scales. What's left should be a hollow pocket.

STEP 2 Spread the tail out and press it flat between two pieces of cardboard covered in wax paper. Use binder clips to keep pressure on the cardboard.

STEP 3 Rub the inside of the pocket with borax laundry powder and then fill up the pocket with expanding plumbing foam. Place the tail in a cool, dry spot to let it set for about three weeks.

STEP 4 Once dry, remove the cardboard and paint the tail to revive the color. Spray paint and acrylic work well. Saw off any excess foam to create a level surface, and glue the tail to a plaque or wood base for display.

ABOUT THE AUTHOR

Joe Cermele started his career in outdoor journalism in 2004, covering fishing tournaments for a local magazine in his home state of New Jersey. In 2005, while attending Rider University, he became an intern at *Salt Water Sportsman* magazine, joining the editorial staff full-time that same year after graduation. In 2008, he moved to sister publication *Field & Stream*, where he was named Fishing Editor in 2011. His writing appears monthly in the magazine, he blogs weekly on the magazine's website, and also hosts and produces *Field & Stream's Hook Shots*, an award-winning web-based fishing show with a punk-rock edge. Cermele has fished all over the country and abroad, but when he's not traveling on assignment, you can find him on his boat pitching tubes to smallmouth bass on the Delaware River, chasing tuna and striped bass off the Jersey coast, or flyfishing for trout in New York's Catskill Mountains.

This book is dedicated to Dave James, an incredible angler and an even more incredible friend. You left us far too soon. Thanks for all the shads.
- J.C.

FIELD & STREAM

In every issue of *Field & Stream* you'll find a lot of stuff: beautiful artwork and photography, adventure stories, wild game recipes, humor, reviews, commentary, and more. That mix is what makes the magazine so great and what's helped it remain relevant since 1895. But at the heart of every issue are the skills. The tips that explain how to use the right lure for every situation, the tactics that help you catch that trophy bass, the lessons that you'll pass on to your kids about the joy of fishing—those are the stories that readers have come to expect from *Field & Stream*.

You'll find a bunch of those skills in this book as well, but there's not enough room in these pages to hold them all. Besides, whether you're new to bass fishing or an old pro, there's always more to learn. You can expect *Field & Stream* to continue teaching you those essential skills in every issue. Plus, there's all that other stuff in the magazine, too, which is pretty great. To order a subscription, visit www.fieldandstream. com/subscription.

FIELDANDSTREAM.COM

When *Field & Stream* readers aren't hunting or fishing, they kill hours (and hours) on fieldandstream.com. And once you visit the site, you'll understand why.

If you enjoy the skills and opinions in this book, there's plenty more online—within our extensive archives of stories from the writers featured here as well as our network of more than 50,000 experts who can answer all of your questions about the outdoors.

At fieldandstream.com, you'll get to explore the world's largest online destination for hunters and anglers. Our blogs, written by leading experts, cover every facet of hunting and fishing, and provide regular content that instructs, enlightens, and always entertains. Our collection of adventure videos contains footage that's almost as thrilling to watch as it is to experience. And our photo galleries include the best wildlife and outdoor photography you'll find anywhere.

Perhaps best of all is the community you'll find online at fieldandstream.com. It's where you can argue with other readers about the best trout fly or the perfect venison chili recipe. It's where you can share photos of the fish you catch and the game you shoot. It's where you can enter contests to win guns, gear, and other great prizes.

And it's a place where you can spend a lot of time. Which is okay. Just make sure to reserve some hours for the outdoors, too.

INDEX

FROM THE AUTHOR

I'd like to thank Mariah Bear, Rob James, Allister Fein, Conor Buckley, and the entire crew at Weldon Owen for keeping my procrastinating self in line throughout the process of working on this book. It was a pleasure to work with all of you. A special thanks also goes to Kayda Norman, who took on the grueling task of compiling fishing material from nearly ten years' worth of *Field & Stream* issues to make this book possible. I'd also like to say thanks to good friend and photographer Tim Romano for lending the art produced by his amazing camera skills to this project. Finally, I'd be remiss if I didn't thank every writer, angler, and fishing guide whose knowledge ended up on these pages. A willingness to share what you've learned on the water makes an angler just as great as do his or her abilities.

CREDITS

All articles by Joe Cermele, with the following exceptions: *Will Brantley:* 45; *Kirk Deeter:* 15, 52; *Mark Hicks:* 4, 14, 46–47, 50, 54, 65, 70; *Mark Hicks, Steve Price & Don Wirth:* 31, 37, 59, 63; *Steven Hill:* 32, 58; *Dave Hurteau:* 61; *Peter B. Mathiesen:* 9; *John Merwin:* 1, 5, 21, 28, 29, 34, 62, 64; *Jerome B. Robinson:* 3, 10, 11, 22, 55; *Slaton L. White:* 36, 68; *Don Wirth:* 23–24, 66, 67

Photographs courtesy of: *Joe Cermele:* 2, 11, 45 (fish); *Eric Engbretson Underwater Photography:* 17, 37, 54, 59; *Cliff Gardner & John Keller:* 6, 61, 63; *Brian Grossenbacher:* TOC, 35; *Todd Huffman:* 1 (w/ exception of curly tail grub); *iStock:* 38, 52; *Alexander Ivanov:* 1 (curly tail grub); *Johanna Lazaro:* 13 (waxworm); *Bill Lindner:* 57; *Rapala Fishing Lures:* 39 (lure); *Travis Rathbone:* 8, 9 (lure); *Tim Romano:* spread title, 28, 34; *Dan Saelinger:* 2, 15, 72; *Shutterstock:* 1, 3, 9 (fisherman, notebook), 11, 13 (w/ exception of golden shiner), 30, 39 (ruler), 40, 50–51, 56, 64–65, 69, 71, credits, imprint; *Uland Thomas:* 13 (golden shiner)

Illustrations courtesy of: *Conor Buckley:* 18, 23, 26, 29, 31, 37, 41, 48, 65, 67; *Hayden Foell:* 15, 38, 25, 36, 56, 66, 70; *Jason Lee:* 4; *Dan Marsiglio:* 7; *Samuel A. Minick:* 33, 44, 68; *Chris Philpot:* 8; *Paula Rogers:* 32, 62; *Mike Sudal:* 50, 53; *Bryon Thompson:* 5; *Lauren Towner:* 46, 49, 37, 55

"The charm of fishing is that it is the pursuit of what is elusive but attainable, a perpetual series of occasions for hope."

—John Buchan

FIELD & STREAM

Editor Anthony Licata
VP, Group Publisher Eric Zinczenko

2 Park Avenue
New York, NY 10016
www.fieldandstream.com

weldon**owen**

President, CEO Terry Newell
VP, Publisher Roger Shaw
Associate Publisher Mariah Bear
Editor Bridget Fitzgerald
Editorial Assistant Ian Cannon
Creative Director Kelly Booth
Art Director Marisa Kwek
Illustration Coordinator Conor Buckley
Production Director Chris Hemesath
Production Manager Michelle Duggan

All of the material in this book was originally
published in *The Total Fishing Manual* by
Joe Cermele and the editors of *Field & Stream*.

Weldon Owen would like to thank Allister Fein for the
original design concept for *The Total Fishing Manual* and
William Mack and Daniel Triassi for additional design help.

© 2013 Weldon Owen Inc.

415 Jackson Street
San Francisco, CA 94111
www.weldonowen.com

Field & Stream and Weldon Owen are divisions of
BONNIER

Library of Congress Control Number on file with
the publisher

ISBN 13: 978-1-61628-679-8
ISBN 10: 1-61628-679-2

10 9 8 7 6 5 4 3 2 1

2013 2014 2015 2016

Printed in China by 1010